From Alcohol To God

From Alcohol To God

catherine findlay

Published by Tablo

Introduction

Dear Reader,

I write this book in poem style as God gave me the Gift after saving me from alcohol's clutches.

I want to share my story and let others with addictions see there is a way out.

I tried to do it myself but kept slipping back.

It wasn't till I was at rock bottom until I cried out for help and God pulled me out the muck.

I bear my soul in my writing in order to help others.

No Friend Of Mine

I once had a friend I used to keep,
Hidden under my pillow when I tried to sleep,
Or, placed in places hidden from view,
The life I lived was so untrue.

That friend started of as a wee acquaintance,
And then years after put me in a trance,
It was no more a friend than the devil himself,
Destroying and maiming bringing down my health.

One day that friend I could no longer keep,
It had blinded and scared me, making me weep,
Thank God for a Friend so kind and true,
He broke that bottle and made my life new.

Pain

Pain! So hard to focus on much else,
Pain! So easy to look inward feeling sorry for yourself,
Pain! Robs you of the joys life has for you,
Pain!Makes it hard to accept God cares for you.
Aah! But what does scripture say?
The joy of the Lord is your strength, all the day,
Overcoming the pain with His Word is the way,
Not easy I know as have struggled each day.
Singing praise through the pain works as well,
Putting moaning aside lifts you from that hell,
So, as hard as it is to look past it to praise,
Let's fight past it and our voices raise,
For God hears and He helps us to help ourselves
Pain! satans tool to lead us astray, God turns to good when
in His Word we delve.

Into Thy Presence

Come we Lord into Thy Presence,
Falling prostrate at Thy feet,
Arise with singing on our lips,
Gather round Your mercy seat.

Day to day we all but flounder,
As Your steady hand does guide,
Bringing us with awe and wonder,
From fear and dreading by Your side.

Guide us through this world of sin,
To bring others hearts to Thee,
Then they also have hearts to win,
And Your faithful Love to see.

Bring us faithfully before You,
As this sick world disappears,
Joyfully we adore You,
Singing praises to Your ears.

Heavens angels ever singing,
Harps resound their cheerful din,
Blessings flow all around us,
As we bow and enter in.

Saved From Drowning In An Alcoholic Sea

Never a day goes by when I do not stop to think,
And thank Thee for Thy care O God that saved me from
the demon drink,
My life is so much better now and I handle stress so well,
Only because of Thy Love for me, and I am glad that I am
here to tell.

Tell of the way Thy healing hand got hold of me,
Pulled me up from drowning in that alcoholic sea,
Yes we move forward and it is not good to dwell,
But times come around where I am led my story to tell.

That sinking sand pulled family down too,
Thy healing hand gave them life anew,
We have so much to be thankful for,
O God, my God Thee I adore.

You fellow sufferers from addictions or pain of different
kinds,
Look up to The Father Who can heal your minds,
It may not come in a flash and may take a lot of hard work
on your part,
But life will be much better and you will have a brand new
start.

Who Am I

Ask me "Who am I today?"
I will tell you with delight.
How I try to walk in Gods' true Way,
Trying to be pleasing in His sight.

Ask me "Who was I before?"
Before I saw The Light?
Never did I need Him more,
When the poison called alcohol did bite.

Ask me to share how bad life was,
Was for others not just myself,
Truthfully I can say what hell I did cause,
Family out in the cold, me hiding in self.

Truly God pulled me out from the mire,
Set me on a Rock.
Brought peace to family and He does not tire,
As now I am on the clock.

Ask me who I am,
As this world comes to an end,
I am His child who has His Word to pass on,
Like all of His children we have little time,
To give others the chance to be free,
And with us worship on bended knee.

Little time left,
All who do not follow,
Are left bereft,
The need for repentance today not tomorrow.
We must do our duty and never fall back or we too will be
left in hell's sorrow.

The Story Behind The Poems

For over 10 long years I drank heavily never having a thought for what I was doing to my family or my body.

At times I would break down in the dark of the night crying out to God for help.

Being brought up in a Christian family I knew what I was doing was so wrong and that made things worse as my heart was fighting itself. However, being in depths of addiction I couldn't stop of my own accord.

The alcohol addiction crept up on me over the years from just social drinking to taking a drink to dull pain that at the time I couldn't understand. Only years down the line did I find out I had been suffering from Post Natal Depression.

After being in the throws of losing my family, marriage and my life I was at my rock bottom.

AA wasn't a help for me, though they have saved many an alcoholic. Alcohol and drug clinic helped a bit but still I kept falling back. Then, in September 2009 I cried and cried all night in my bed till I had no more tears and fell onto my knees out of bed.

There and then God answered my plea and I never touched another drink. I went through horrid cold turkey and have been left with a nauseating feeling when smelling alcohol.

From all this has come the Gift of poetry writing. I make no apology that all my poems/prose has a Christian theme as I can only give God the glory. He saved my life and turned my families lives around too.

These poems and my story I hope and pray will help others

struggling with addiction and let them see there is a way out. It won't be easy, I still had to put the work in, but God helped make it happen.

What Is Holding You Down?

Ten years ago I could have been dead.
Ten years ago I felt nothing but dread.
 Nine years ago God pulled me from the mire,
And giving Him my thanks I will never tire.

What is holding you down today?
What is pulling you away?
Fear and doubt, worry and stress?
God has you covered, He'll fix the mess.

Pray to Him always ask Him to stay,
Close beside you all the day,
He never strays from your side,
And in His care you always abide.

Strength To Bear

Dear Lord, this pain overwhelms me,
But I try to push on through.
Right now I need to meet with Thee,
I know Your promise is true.

Lord, I really don't like moaning,
But today has been so bad,
Lord, hear my yearning,
Give me back the life I had.

But as I sit here and write,
It is not my life but Yours.
Just give me strength to bear it,
Live not for myself but You.

In The Middle Of The Night

What do you do in the middle of the night,
When time goes slow and morning's out of sight?
Be it pain, distress with life,
Someone's words that cut you with a knife.

All those thoughts keeping you awake,
Needing sleep for sanity's sake.
Then dear friends what I like to do,
Is get out of bed and on knees seek His heart so true.

Not every time, will sleep come,
But a peace will be given from The Holy One.
O Lord, Whose Love is unconditional,
Give us Your Peace and life eternal.

Beautiful Love

Beautiful and unconditional is Your Love for me,
What Your eye sees in me is a mystery,
For out of human frailty,
Your Love turns into royalty.

Through twists and turns of human life,
You pull us out of troubles and strife,
Set us up upon The Rock,
So, of our lives we can take stock.

Lord, we bless You for Your Love and Care,
And from that we want to share,
So others will see too,
How You made our lives anew.

My Place In Heaven

I am dreaming of my place in Heaven,
Where in Christ Jesus I shall rest,
No more worry and no more scurry,
Just peace and a great contentedness.

I am dreaming of my place in Heaven,
At God's right hand my rest shall be,
All earths madness and great sadness,
Will be forever a distant memory.

I am dreaming of my place in Heaven,
Christ gave His life to let it be so,
Thank You Father, for life ever after,
In Your footsteps I will go.

From Far Away She Found God's Peace

From far away she travelled, to sit at her Kings' feet,
Looking for the comfort she would get at His Mercy Seat,
So many years a lost soul was she,
Travelling far to be set free.

Through many a quagmire did she come,
From a far away place, to The Holy One,
A weeping sadness strewn on her face,
All she sought was her Father God's Grace.

A Grace she felt she didn't deserve,
But down on her knees she wanted to serve,
She had heard of that peace no one else could give,
And in her heart she wanted Him to live.

At last that peace to her did come,
The greatest Love from The Holy One,
Her heart was filled to overflowing,
The sadness gone, her face a-glowing.

The peace that only our Father can give,
Had now let her see what it was like to live,
Walking close at the Father's side,
No longer crying or needing to hide.

Do Not Be Alone

Though your troubles may overwhelm you,
Though you cannot see a way out,
Look to God our Father,
Check out His Word,
For freeing you from these burdens is what He is all about.

Of course there is so much more to God our Saviour,
Nothing is impossible for Him,
There is nothing in your life He doesn't care about,
No matter how bad our sin.

As long as we come humbly on bended knee,
Broken heartedly,
Leaving all our sin behind,
He will give us New Life,
Come repentantly.

God gave me so many chances,
My sin overwhelmed my life,
Even I, He lifted up,
Let me drink again from His Loving Cup.

Nobody needs to fight this world alone,
Just to Him your sins atone.

In The Midst Of Troubles

In the midst of your troubles God is there,
He will never leave you as He cares,
You cannot see a way forward but He can,
Put your trust in the Father's hands.

Your heart is so heavy with all that's going on,
Look up to our Father this battle He's won,
Thank Him in all things and praise His Name,
Then these troubles will not remain.

So dear friend remember this well,
Even when this seems a living hell,
God will give you comfort through it all.

Let's Be Ready

Through days of mixed emotions,
At times so hard to bear,
I search my heart for comfort,
And find my Lord there.

The twists and turns of daily life,
The highs and the lows.
I find the peace and contentment,
From the seed His Love sows.

Oh my Glorious Saviour,
Loving such a sinner as I,
I bow my head in wonder,
And Your Name from my lips I cry.

These days are moving faster,
The time is fleeting by,
Our Lord is coming very soon,
Let's be ready!

Times Of Doubt

We find ourselves in times of doubt,
When it feels more is piled upon us to worry about,
We cannot concentrate on what we are doing,
For all we see are our worries growing,
I know and you know where the answer lies,
In the hour of prayer looking into our Father's eyes,
O God in Heaven send down to us,
Your comfort and help from above,
For only You can bring us Home,
To the place no more our minds will roam.

The Miracle Of Grace

I don't know why You want me after all I've said and
done.
I wonder why You saved me from from the journey I was
on,,
These things went through my mind when I was too blind
to see,
The miracle of Your Grace and Love is why You saved me.

So many times I've wandered so far away from You,
Getting deeper and further away from Your Love so true,
Yet, each and every time I fall,
You pick me up and stand me tall.

Adonai, forever I am grateful,
You have shown Your heart so full,
Of Mercy and Grace for a sinner like me,
I bow down and worship on bended knee.

We do not always follow You the way that we were
taught,
And neither do we talk the way that we ought,
But You forgive us every time we fail to make the grade,
And I for one am grateful for You catch me when I've
strayed.

You Pull Me Through

Ever nearer on my journey I will come to You,
Following Your pathway willingly , the road so narrow and
true,
I do not truly understand what lies ahead for me,
Only that by Faith I walk until Thy face I see.

Your Love lifts me from despair, this hurtful sin filled
world,
I fight each day to stay afloat with my armour and my
Sword,
It doesn't always work the way that I would want it to,
Your will not mine be done O Lord, Thy will so true.

So Father on this day I have struggled but You have pulled
me through,
No problem or hurt is too great for You,
To turn around and teach me,
And You will always reach me,
And let me see You care and are always there,
Waiting to save me from this world that doesn't care.

True friends You always send,
To help this bleeding heart mend,
Thank You that You will always be,
The greatest Friend to me.

Help Me Lord

What can I do Lord?
I feel helpless, lost,
Don't think anyone cares,
These feelings inside,
Are beyond compare,
Feel worthless, in despair,
Can see only one way out,
So much hurt,so much doubt,
Please help!

My child, I hear you,
You are not alone,
You are loved more than you know,
Let all your feelings out,
No more fear, no more doubt,
Trust Me to lift your burden,
I have prepared you a seat beside Me,
And when the time is right,
I will call you too the Light,
But until then,
Rest, fear not, trust in Me.

God Changes Lives

Life has it's moments,
It's twists and turns,
Endless troubles and dead ends,
Trying to change I'd end up burnt,
Going nowhere, need a friend,
Jesus, Lord, Saviour, You are that friend,
You came and saved me,
When I was ready to end,
End it all, the grief the pain,
The tears falling like pouring rain,
Friends and family I hurt so bad,
Losing the trust that they once had,
But Jesus,now You changed all that,
The trust is returning,
And my heart is yearning,
For the full trust and love I once had.
Thank You Jesus for never leaving,
Even through all the deceiving,
I cling to Your promise,
Of everlasting love,
Your child has returned,
Rescued, saved,
No longer that way of life I crave,
God show through me,
The hope, the change,
We find through Thee,
A down and out, an alcoholic, drug addict,

All feel lost, alone,
But I know Lord no matter what,
You will pick us up if we just ask.

On The Edge

Standing at the edge of the abyss,
Wanting to jump, there must be more than this?
I don't understand,
I need Your help Lord,
Catch me before I leap and leave this land.

The mess I've made,
The lying games I played,
Stealing, lying, just to get,
The next drink to oblivion.

Crying myself to sleep,
Hating, feel only disgust for me,
Supposed to be model daughter,
Minister Dad, No I just bad,
Bad,sad,great life I had,
Till ugly drink made it stink.

Lord, from the brink,
You caught me,
No longer I think,
Of that person I was,
I'm renewed, refined,
Oh God divine,
Your child returns.

Take My Hand

Lord of my life,
Today I give,
All of my heart,
So that I may live,
As one with You,
Being ever true,
To Your commands,
Please take my hand,
And lead me through,
All pain and worry,
To that bright light,
Of peace and joy,
My life no longer a maze,
Doing right in Your gaze,
Thank You for showing,
That awesome love,
Never ending, never failing.

Up, Not Down

No longer do I stay down long,
My mood You always change,
Into my mind You sing sweet songs,
It's time to turn the page.

Always be positive,
No need for gloom and despair,
Look up, not down,
Never wear a frown,
Come closer to me,
Cling to my love so true.

So Father, thank You from the bottom of my heart,
As usual You came through,
Let's all together take heart from this,
Cling steadfast to our Lord so true.

Praise Him Always

"Praise Him in the morning
Praise Him in the evening
Praise Him in the noontide
And the break of day!"

Lord we get bogged down,
With worries and cares
Forgetting that You alone are forever there.
We feel sad and lonely,
But all this needn't be,
As we can praise and pray all night and day,
Worries fly away, cares disappear,
Only when we praise,
And bring You ever near.

So Heavenly Father, Lord of Love,
We greet You with our hearts of love,
You fill us with Your Truth Divine,
Reminding us to let Your Light shine,
Praise and prayer all day we bring,
And songs of Love from You above,
Bring Hope and Peace and Joy,
All sadness gone we will hold on,
Lord of our hearts we come!

Light At The End Of The Tunnel

There is a Light at the end of the tunnel,
You may not think so but it is there,
Our Lord Jesus stands before us,
And His Love is beyond compare.

Through struggles His arms are around us,
Through pain, His heart takes it all,
Our life will be so much better,
If we learn to take that call.

Lord Jesus, You are just awesome,
My heartache is all but gone,
It could've been taken much sooner,
But took a while for me to see what was wrong.

Spend more time reading the Bible,
Live a prayerful life every day,
God's Word will speak,
And truly show you the Way.

To be in a better position,
We have to go through the pain,
But God never gives us too much to handle,
And through it we can gain,

Perfect peace and contentment,
A loving caring heart,

To be as Christ-like as we can be,
What a feeling I will not part.

Forgiveness

Forgiveness is not easy,
We all know that,
But to walk the Christian way,
It is not fiction but fact.

God tells us to forgive,
As we have been forgiven.
Past hurts and pains God takes away,
If we truly forgive and walk His way.

Sometimes there are things we know we did wrong,
Truly repenting is all we can do,
God never remembers our wrongs,
Unfortunately close people do.

I am writing this down to remind me,
That no matter what others may say,
God knows my real heart,
And I repented and made a fresh start.

So whatever hurt I feel now,
I give to my God up above,
And I ask His hand upon those,
Who I truly and deeply love.

Give me much stronger courage,
To take a stand against all that is thrown,

Be confident in His love for me,
And continue as I am not alone.

Lost Souls

So many lost and broken people,
Living in the world today,
Not a lot to make them happy,
Its time we act, not just say.

Lord, let us be enabled,
To encourage and entrust,
All Your lost and lonely people,
To come back to You, it is a must.

There, but by Thy grace go I,
Been there, done that, then You walked by,
Took me from that miry pit,
No longer now am scared to die.

So with all our experience together,
Knowing what we know today,
Give our time, our health, our wealth,
Bring God's people home to stay.

Fill Me

The calmness of my heart,
Is a new feeling for me,
To sit with You in the quiet,
Just listening, letting You be....

Letting You be in my head,
Filling my heart with Your love,
Such beautiful sounds and thoughts,
You send down upon me from above.

Lord, I feel You changing me,
I want more and more,
Pour out Your anointing oil,
And allow my heart to sore.

Keep filling me Lord,
And each new day,
I will speak from Your Word,
And honour You in all I do and say.
AMEN

Be Encouraged

What a joy is in my heart Lord,
I hope it is plain to see,
The smile on my face, the glint in my eye,
Can you all see the change in me?

No longer the timid wee creature,
Hiding behind the drink,
You gave me a joy and I am sure,
I have changed all I do, say, and think.

My children have got their mum back,
The confidence they have has grown,
Not only am I on the right track,
Your seed in them is sown.

So then, I just want to encourage,
Those folks struggling inside,
Your time will come though it may seem an age,
You can do it with God at your side.

Soaking In Your Presence Lord

Soaking in Your presence Lord,
Is such a joy to me,
Shutting of the busy world,
To rest and listen to Thee.

When lying or sitting quietly,
No distractions found,
You come into my heart silently,
Calming, loving, sound.

A little light music playing in the background,
Helps to relax my mind,
All the busyness of the day,
Disappears and Your grace abounds.

So, Lord,thank You for teaching me,
How to relax in Thee,
And giving me security,
My life belongs to Thee.

Peace, Calm, Reflection

Peace, calm, reflection,
Something we all need,
Keeping close to Jesus,
And on His Word should feed.

Our hearts get filled with nonsense,
Picking up dirt along the way,
A calm reflection, a heart at rest,
Cleanses and feeds us for a new day.

Whenever things surround us,
Worry, dread or fear,
Look for that peace and calm reflection,
Showing us that God is here.

Go about your business,
Daily pray for peace,
Calm reflection follows,
God is our release.

The Hand Of God

There's a hand that crosses the hugest of divides,
Doesn't make a difference or take sides,
The hand will right all wrongs for you,
Taking care of all you do.

The hand of God will always be,
The first act of kindness that you see,
The person lending a listening ear,
The hand on your shoulder, taking away fear.

Never be afraid to reach out to God's hand,
For with you He will always stand,
His hand will pull you from the mire,
No matter how deep or dire.

Be bold and take the hand of God,
Whether it be from reading His Word,
Or from a helping hand of a friend,
Gods reaching hand will never end.

I know the time may seem so slow,
Your life for years is your foe,
But Gods hand is there,
Believe in His timing for He really does care.

Trusting In You

Thank You Lord for saving me,
Laying down your life so selflessly,
Such pain and suffering You did bear,
Dear Jesus I draw near.

No longer am I downcast, distraught,
New life from your pain was sought,
I shall live my life anew,
Take up my cross and follow You.

Trusting on you every day,
Never again going my own way,
I lift up my hands Lord,
My lips shall utter no bad word.

Patience, compassion, kindness and caring,
Let that be part of my calling,
Thanks on my lips to You each day,
Lord, thank you, I walk in Your way.

Higher Ground

Teach me to live on higher ground,
Fill my heart with joy,
The joy of living safe and sound,
In Your arms and safe employ.

Let my heart rejoice in you, O Lord,
Full of praise and glee,
For walking with You and reading Your Word,
Is the best and safest place to be.

Though slings and arrows fly at me,
My heart no longer worries,
As straight to Your arms I will flee,
And with You I will tarry.

My heart O Lord, is on higher ground,
What joy is in my heart,
The peace and comfort I have found,
Lord, from You I will not part.

Lead Me Father

I trust my Father's leading,
He never lets me down,
He leads me through the good and bad and onwards to the
Crown.
Oh yes that Crown of life shall be mine,
And with His Son and He I shall come to dine.
Oh joyfully my heart beats,
It soars o'er land and sea,
Till in the end I gain that prize,
I'll be at Home with Thee.
How wonderful Your love for me, such a sinner,
You've turned life all around and made me a winner,
I've won the greatest ever prize.
To You my hands do rise \0/

Jesus, The Perfect Pick Me Up

Lord, Thank You that you love us,
No matter how we feel,
One minute our mood is so good,
The next we just want to brood.

The sadness can attack us,
Take us unawares,
Brings us to our knees,
But You are always there.

Your promises hold so true,
We know we can rely on You,
So Lord Jesus, You are the perfect "pick me up",
We will drink from Your loving cup.

Look Forward

Look into my eyes, what do you see?
Sadness of the past or the happiness that is me?
I cannot dwell on the years gone before,
I only look forward to what God has in store.

After He brought me from a wordly dis...ease,
When He took me broken from my knees,
He gave me a chance to start anew,
And He will do just that for you.

No hardship or trial can hold you back,
With God on your side you nothing lack,
The strength to go on when before you failed,
I trusted God and my heart sailed.

Acknowledgements

I want to thank my family, both my side and Douglas's, for standing by me through the painful times I caused them.

Also more especially to Douglas who endured such a tough time, and my kids Laura and Euan. They all suffered a great deal with my alcoholism.

To my closest friends from school and nursing, who are family too, who also stayed the course.

To my friends from Tranent Parish Church, The Fraser Centre and others I know who all prayed me through and helped us as a family. And those special friends who helped me especially through your dedication and friendship.

I know I would not be here today if it had not been for the power of prayer and God grabbing me from the depths of despair I was in.

Addiction of any kind hurts the family perhaps more ,as we as addicts cannot see what we are doing till we hit the bottom and need help.

I hope and pray anyone reading this book of heartfelt poems is helped, and will come to see God comes through for even the most messed up person.

The Lord bless you and keep you,

The Lord make His face to shine upon you,

And be gracious unto you.

The Lord lift up His countenance upon you,

And give you peace. Amen.

Alcoholism and any addiction not only hurts the addict but the whole family!